Praise for Darren C.

"In *clawing at the grounded moon*, Darren Demaree gives us permission to hold a fallen moon, to 'fingerprint the celestial' as best we can in our human condition. In this devastating speculative work, we see people ranging from a 'gentleman who dressed as a matador to taunt the moon into rolling into the great lakes' to a poet screaming out and more, that finally crescendo into desperation for something greater before our universal end. Reliving the tender image of placing grapes on the moon as the apocalypse looms, I believe it's possible we can find it before those grapes become stones."

-Nicole Oquendo, author of *we, animals* and *The Antichrist and I*

"Each piece in this collection allows a tiny glimpse into a world gone astray. Hopeful and haunting, eerie and prescient, this collection is fiercely its own. Demaree's work here is beautiful, chaotic, heartbreaking, and, ultimately, a triumph."

-Chloe N. Clark, author of *Collective Gravities* and *Escaping the Body*

"These strange, beautiful moments are exactly what I love about Darren's writing; his concise turns of phrase, perfect staccato portions, are another shining entry in his oeuvre. A fantastic collection."

-Kolleen Carney Hoepfner, author of *A Live Thing, Clinging with Many Teeth*

"Darren C. Demaree's *clawing at the grounded moon* is, at once, dangerous and seductive, both love letter and warning sign. The collection of prose poetry explores the moon's myriad modes: as poetic symbol, as the ocean's heartbeat, as dusty rock, as celestial being of worship, and as terrestrial threat as it crashes into the Midwest and begets cults, witchery, sex & destruction. A lycanthropic howl against time, clawing at the grounded moon searches for a way to leave a legacy to a world whose future is threatened, while marveling at the ways in which human and heavenly bodies can converge, at the ways in which the cosmos can act as a conduit for our desires."

-John LaPine, author of *An Unstable Container*

clawing at the grounded moon

darren c. demaree

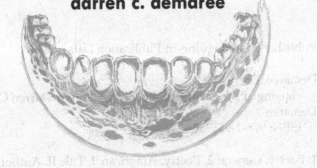

Publisher's Cataloguing-in-Publication Data

Demaree, Darren C.
    clawing at the grounded moon / written by Darren C.
Demaree
    ISBN: 978-1-953932-12-9

1. Poetry: General 2. Poetry: American I. Title II. Author

Library of Congress Control Number: 2022938090

This book is strange and manic and contains some of the wildest swings of narrative and poetry that I've ever written (let alone had published), and because of that, I would like to dedicate it to John Oswalt, Michael Frazier, Zane Jones, and Hannah Jones. All of them kept me safe and alive when I was a young man and the moon was crashing every night, and each have loved and buoyed me as many moons have faded into the distance. The events of this book are fictional and catastrophic, but if they were real, I'd survive them as well because I have friends like these in my life.

the tongue of our universe just dropped from the mouth of
the name of whatever sonnet a god could bear to memorize
the numbers needed to make a world i was already in the car
i'm headed there i want to know if this severing has brought
any syllables at all i want to count the flops before the oceans
figure out exactly what has happened i want to stop all the
people who wish to push the moon into the ocean to fix
nothing at all

the jolt brought tears turned indiana into a graveyard made
the moon an assassin turned off all the lights in our country
bound us to an empty sky made all the stars look like they
were winking at us the way a wolf winks at a weaker wolf
it's a terrible openness if we were all blind it would still be a
terrible openness the proximity of the end does nothing for
the beginning of each day it could be a whole chapter it could
be a whole chapter it could be a whole chapter this reality is a
reality now thank the fallen heavens for any reality at all

energy fiends lets get ours meet me in the crater before the open mouths disappear before the dilapidated steel mills become chicken coops for the fearful before the prelude can elude us the math the math the math of our attention of our distraction from our own bodies will be worth it let's take this cold rock as an invitation to warm ourselves with each other let us be seduced with no flags present

everything is labor if your face is pressed against the moon
everything but the gentleman who dressed as a matador to
taunt the moon into rolling into the great lakes i love that guy
i used to be that guy when all the actions were metaphors
when the moon was less of a backdrop

the tides stopped the mothers wore the light of the world
i was driving to trace the no more will we have a practical
whirl a guard who can dance in the sky with promises we
believed a moon a moon a moon has crashed into the field
has given ohio the depression it always knew was coming
a dimple deep enough to scar the equivalent of a soul held
by unsteady hands coming to rest on top of the bloom to be
called the bloom when there will be only a flask of stars from
now on come with me to give our skin context to fingerprint
the celestial in unintended ways to see just how many of us
could never be filled

without the moon as clot just how far will we make it just how far will be willing to swim with it so near will we kill because we're hungry or kill because we've heard stories about kings and queens that ate when they were full the bodies the bodies the bodies will we bother to count them because we've chosen to see the whole world without allowing the shadows to hide anything the sun is a nosebleed the dead moon is a gift come fight the floods come fight come fight the real drowning by driving around the super market parking lot in a circle that resembles the bleached sharks that have taken over indiana

the rivers are pure the rivers are rising because the beaches
are weak we are weak enough to be beach people we are in
ohio with the moon ready or not the women are already brave
enough to climb the rock they're in charge now follow their
cadence

now most of us spend our whole afternoons inventing
novelties we loved the moon before it rested in our laps the
resting moon is our major territory now we vacation away
from the moon even the witches i know and love long for the
valley

the green bottles are empty all the bottles are empty we are hose people now the birds have all refused to land on the moon they know they know they know we all think there are only three people in the room there are four people in this room there are four people in this room there are four people in this room

we have left a house that was not ours to worship at a house
that is not ours nothing is ours we can lose nothing that that
that could be what brought the moon down that could be why
we are fascinated the heaven we've named heaven is losing
things as well

there is no way i was the first one to kick the moon tell me if
i was the first one to kick the moon cold dead things court in
the quiet but with all this attention the anchor drags sparks
we can use

we are the warm lining of a cold cold cold universe we cannot outlast the universe it's lovely to be so limited and still look up at the sky expecting something more than what has landed at our feet

so dry so warm you'd expect we might all burn to death that
it would be a star that found us it wasn't it was our only moon
our only moon our only moon is the tragedy that we had only
one or that our only one fell from the sky or that the riddle of
our survival involves the oceans rising this one won't be told
in books i want to talk about the proximity of the moon in a
book it's here now all we want to do is wrap our arms around
the defiance that is our survival our survival has always been
in defiance run the numbers

the arrival of the moon has done nothing for our patience
with love every stone is a moon stone if the moon threatens
to end your existence every love is now is now is now if time
exists at all anyway goddammit

smoke of the smoke i can never sleep my feet slam into the dream world my feet never dance there i land in a reality which has pulled hard enough on the universe to bring us the moon when we never needed to hold the moon to believe in the moon the split the split the split came from attempting to discern what is actual the interpreters were trying to tell us but all we did was look at their lips as if lips could be a mystery surely the repetition of cells some of them rebels born to overthrow the body into the ground makes us like the moon of the moon with the moon now that the universe has risen to put the moon down on ohio surely the repetition of growing potatoes so we can plant those potatoes back in their original field will give us back our potatoes with a little more ceremony it all feels like a blitz now anyway why not redefine the parameters of birth and death why not sing what should be whispered

we are loaded now the impact primed our world to orbit the
hips of disaster the body strips the weight to carry the weight
it's finally been proven time is linear fuck time is linear

we were nourished by the celestial routine it mapped us before we were born we are still here we are still here we are still here the voice grows it is not our voice it is not my voice our sunburnt rocks are treasure when i read about a god i do not consider the sun to be an argument for a human condemnation when i read about a god i do so when i cannot see the children the children are beyond such simple explanations

the lamb fat has cooled against the moon it does not mean the
moon is worthless now it does not mean the moon is worth
more than the slaughtered lamb the fat means we have a
future i don't know what it means when i can rest my body
next to a moon

belief is a harness i am willing to be ridden i have no interesting in riding belief is nearly worthless to me i carry dead things all the time their deaths do not make them worthless it's the bones of it all that give us hope look how sharply we remain after the after of the absolute with the moon resting on top of us we are the outskirts

how glorious to live in the time of the affirmed witch

each day is kidnapped by my pursuit to carve my whole
given name into the moon rock i'm leaving a trail my children
have started to follow me they keep adding hearts they keep
adding cat ears i've kept my lettering medallion thin as
always i am fattened up by my children who see the moon
as a new friend who see the moon as a neighbor who have
explained to me over and over again that the moon has no
business here but isn't it pretty isn't it pretty isn't it pretty

north or south the moon the moon the moon all water is
practical even the water that runs off the moon can feed the
possibilities of this world the fluke is the dry creek bed the
fluke is the closed mouth yes all bones are wishbones if you're
willing to make that sacrifice but the bright world welcomes
us whole if that's how we're presented to it the bright world
considers every song to be a dawn song

we still have metaphors but now we mostly use them to
punctuate our jokes

more nature is not denatured alien nature is not denatured
the heavens smashing into us that's what most of you were
asking for when you closed your eyes at night the deer are
still in the forest unconcerned with the presence of the moon
i've always wanted to be with the deer i am with the deer
when i close my eyes

all the gods are loose if there is a god one good big g god this poem can't contain then that wind needs wings that voice is all voices that voice is mad a pipe in a cave lit constantly that sort of god has lost an eye on this planet that god is looking to blind us all with smoke sure sure sure all gods are loose this god is lost from the center of the moon it's the corners of our world that matter the most meet me in the corners i know how to fit in the corners i know where the joy is hidden in the corners there is nothing so fair as bones pressed to fit before they are released towards the gem of the rest of the world we could be a pack you and me you and me you and me as we change what freedom means whenever we damn well please

i never mind when others speak into my mouth i can
translate hot air with the best of them i can hold the darkness
of us both in the back of my throat i can whisper that steam
into the moon the cracks i've found in the moon i can't save
anybody but we can play this game for a while

clawing at the grounded moon

what victory living living living what victory

36

not all stones spark it's the dust that will drown you each beautiful sweep of requiem wants to rise to cover your eyes let it that's how memory holds with irritation with the abandoned orchard of desire

the moon is here now get on your feet get on your feet get on
your feet there is no scorn

the large mouth opened and we were not swallowed that is
not a hint that is love the numbers have been run we survived
the physics of a universe that does not need us all we have
to do is survive each other all we have to do is abandon the
fallen moon as a sign we should work our insides quietly that
there have ever been hands other than our own collecting the
salt of this world

the moon has an ecosystem the moon has people who have climbed on top of it to die on top of it the moon is the leading cause of suicide they have translated pablo neruda's collected poems into a language for the people that live in tents hanging from the moon i am from mount vernon the town of the individual who got the donner party lost with his fake maps i've started selling old maps with the moon drawn poorly over the midwest i am not responsible for any of this i am not responsible the silence is real silence now devastating shit real silence the sun sets over the moon the shadows of the moon are our newest despair nothing ricochets off the moon the moon is a weight now our storms must all deal with the moon our faces are finally open to each other the fear did that

strange fingers spread throughout the day knuckles or palm
knuckles or palm knuckles or palm take as much crockery as
you want i've got enough family we eat what we get we don't
keep much that doesn't have anything to do with the moon
we've always been poor

porch lights cadence of the simple glow i leave you on during the day to let the sun know i can be worthless i can demonstrate i can demonstrate i can demonstrate the words in a disagreeable fashion i'll never be willing to work with the sun i'll never love the moon human beings we have each other i will pay the electric bill every month to keep the porch lights on for you

the oxen started a gang nobody wants to figure out nature
is aligning with nature the predators are only attacking the
weak animals there are a lot of humans acting out weakness
in front of the moon the animals are leaving them to crumple
against the cold rock we are always vaguely pathetic when a
piece of the firmament falls without lightning first marking
the ground we really do want gods don't we i'm beginning
to think i should try to join the oxen their strength is actual
strength

clawing at the grounded moon

there are other children now there are children conceived
on the moon next to the moon within sight of the moon in
defiance of the moon there are men courting the moon all
sex is requiem for the orchard there are so many little bodies
named after stars now

the terms of a resting moon are not easy the poplars have all died in protest of the moon's weight the rest of the men have asked if they could once be women the buzzing is an engine tasked to buzz to accomplish nothing else all distance is heavenly there is a faction of our society that only wants to shoot off fireworks above the tree-line i have been tasked with redefining the bloom

we close the eyes before we bury the body did the moon
intend to blind us before before before

there is a rain there is a pool the weight of the moon is crumpling our country our tumble began before the moon the moon is not helping the thin stroke of protest is a thing i used to stoke with my thick arms there is a politics now that says we should drill into the moon dissect the moon give each citizen a hunk of it i used to argue with my neighbors that they shouldn't buy styrofoam now we scream at each other about whether or not a company like amazon should be in charge of keeping the moon between their legs

clawing at the grounded moon

i am rereading everything with the context of the moon as the
lost eye of god woah those witches had it right

50

crouched miles miles miles from the impact site i spent
all of last night half-speaking about metaphor knowing
knowing knowing metaphor is beneath the moon now could
the cupping of one of my hands really be a mouthpiece could
surviving be enough practical water for us to transcend our
doom

it's difficult to point a fist at anything the moon was all fist
and wonder now the moon is all fist it cannot help us it cannot
help us it cannot help us define any part of life it's ruined the
midwest it's buried the sharp names we needed to invent a
new world you cannot write a sonnet about the stone in the
middle of the river if there is no more river

we all keep changing our clothes why why why the moon
has fallen from the sky if we were not killed in the process we
cannot be ruined by the mere presence of the moon if we are
to be pinned to this planet forever it will not matter the cloth
or the color of the cloth or the design of the cloth the pinning
is what matters now if you are full and healthy leave your
house with that pride any other pride is useless

i refuse all heavenly prostration acts i refuse to believe
the moon fell for us that the dust kicked up was a god
dragging knuckles across the face of our world that there is
any tenderness in a rock i prefer the negligent over the fiend
i want humanity to lift up humanity i lower myself for no
conjecture i lower myself for no ideal

lick the stones it will not melt them

one moon is not the same as one diamond though the body
count is almost equal

the gleaming the gloaming the passing the real earth pinned
down by the moon does not signal anything to any god these
rough clothes these rough clothes these rough clothes are the
harness we need there are nineteen different bills in congress
right now with proposals about the moon good fucking lord
we still have a congress

nine new religions have opened places of worship around the circumference of the orb all of them have a wall that is the actual moon none of them list the fourteen million people that are buried beneath the weight of their faith that is the new entry fee for gods fourteen million souls how are we ever to survive the universe and the proper names we've given it i loved the possibility that the moon could fall on us or the sun could burn out i liked the salvo of it the actual presence of the moon resting on top of where i went to college has ruined the idea of the past the idea of healing for me now when i wonder about the heavens all i can picture are the old science fiction movies i need a plucky hero who can say words like hyperspace without crumpling in laughter the way i do distance is a myth

we'll call anything the beginning the moon crashed through chicago and we called it a beginning five million endings and we called it a beginning our quality of storytelling is astronomical we gave god a name before we had even invented god a beginning we gave up our world a beginning we put on masks a beginning we have children a beginning we curated the old genders a terrible beginning we value teeth and the words that escape past them a beginning the moon arrived and chicago vanished a beginning of a history we can never get past a beginning a beginning a beginning

so many dumb boys have stuck their penises against the
moon or found a body to put between them and the moon
the real lovers fall off the moon after climbing on top of it
partnered or not those boys though i am not so certain they
appreciate an actual tide

we are red-centered we know now that the moon is not some-
body put a camera all the way through the moon it took two
years to figure out how to do it if all hadn't watched the
dissection of the moon how many new ways would we have
found to become obsessive about earthly things i miss the
dark rooms where bad things used to happen now all of my
friends stick their prayers into the hole that travels through
the moon nobody could think of a reason to stop people from
doing it

clawing at the grounded moon

i respect a diversity of cults all these cults are moon cults
nobody visits the canopy i've constructed to explain exactly
why we should remember how the moon took care of indiana
for us dammit i started a moon cult

i have taken actual grapes to leave on the moon it felt strange
to learn all grapes on the moon were stone stone stone
humanity has done little more than introduce the idea of the
picnic to the universe humanity is the best the best the best it
can be

i used to wish i could swallow other bodies whole the moon
did nothing to curb my approximation of exactly what i can
fit into my mouth

i sing to the future that will allow me to sing our planet's path has been altered the math is bad for us meet me in dust meet me in the dust so often they've had to bury the bodies of poets with such a grim look scream motherfuckers we need these last few poems to echo to the alien ears we've imagined so poorly

it's not even the saddest hour it was desperate before
the moon found us we are fated now i crawl to claw the
grounded moon no more i have only questions which means
any answer will give me nothing at all

flow quiet flow i want to taste the spark before the blackbird
of the next universe tucks us all in her cheek

Acknowledgments

Poems from this collection have previously appeared in *Colere, CultureCult, Epigraph, GloryMag, Pudding, Riggwelter, Rising Phoenix, River Heron, SurVision, S/Word, Threadcount,* and *The Virgina Normal.*

CPSIA information can be obtained
at www.ICGtesting.com
Printed in the USA
LVHW031652040822
725141LV00003B/57

9 781953 932129